Debunking Common
Bitcoin
Criticisms

AN ANALYSIS OF THE MAIN
BITCOIN MYTHS AND CRITICISMS

ALVARO SUAREZ

ISBN 979-83-9248-7-752

To the Bitcoin community

CONTENT

PREFACE

If something is evident, it is that Bitcoin does not leave anyone indifferent. Bitcoin has a large number of supporters and detractors, whose positions are sometimes based on solid arguments, and at other times based solely on headlines and persistent myths.

In my case, as a strong supporter of the benefits of Bitcoin, I believe it is important not to ignore the criticism of those who have opposing opinions. It is good to listen to them and analyze them to understand how much truth there is in them. If a criticism cannot be supported with arguments and evidence, it may contain some truth. Bitcoin is a science and we should not make it a leap of faith or dogma.

> *Extraordinary Claims Require Extraordinary Evidence*
>
> (Sagan, 1979)

The truth is that Bitcoin has been the subject of misunderstandings and a multitude of criticisms and unfair judgments since the publication of its white paper fourteen years ago. Fully understanding Bitcoin is complex, as it combines very diverse areas of knowledge that take us out of our comfort zone.

As they say, Bitcoin is a rabbit hole that, once inside, we don't know where it will lead us and we may never stop learning new things. Faced with this situation, there are those who face it with humility, decide to give it a chance and dedicate the time that Bitcoin needs and deserves, and there are those who do not. My experience tells me that those who decide to give it this chance end up becoming supporters instead of detractors.

> *Writing a description for this thing for general audiences is bloody hard. There's nothing to relate it to.*
>
> (Nakamoto, Re: Slashdot Submission for 1.0, 2010)

After thousands of hours of study, I wrote the book *The Fundamentals of Bitcoin* in 2022 with the aim of shortening the learning curve for those who are beginning to discover this invention, providing a 360-degree vision of what Bitcoin is. And while writing the book, I considered the possibility of including a chapter dedicated to analyzing the main criticisms that Bitcoin receives. Finally, I decided not to do it because despite relying on objective data, it has a certain degree of subjectivity and uncertainty, which makes it impossible to reach a clear and forceful conclusion.

Although I finally did not include said chapter, the desire to carry it out and offer it to the world did not disappear. As a result of that desire, this second book arises, in which some of the already popular criticisms and myths that surround this invention are analyzed. Criticisms that have been repeated and answered on multiple occasions and from different points of view. With this book, I try to understand the claims from one side and the other, for and against, and create my own point of view.

I hope that these analyzes serve to provide some clarity and, who knows, even to "convert" some detractors into supporters. This will not always be possible and we will only be able to say Nakamoto's now famous phrase: "If you don't believe me or don't understand, I don't have time to try to convince you, I'm sorry."

In any case, I wanted to take a moment to personally thank you for your support and for taking the time to read my work. It's readers like you who encourage me to keep creating content like this. If you have acquired this book by paying for it, I thank you and ask you a favor, when you finish it leave a comment or evaluation where you have acquired it. If, on the other hand, you got it for free and you think it deserves it, you can help with a small bitcoin donation. Any amount, however small, will be greatly appreciated.

You can donate with Lightning on the page:

https://getalby.com/p/asuarezbravo

To donate with bitcoin on-chain use the following address or QR:

bc1q2regp07uyk70la4rarcp0nf6jkjzj788dtccww

Once again, thank you so much for reading my book and for considering making a donation. Your support means a lot to me.

1

BITCOIN HAS NO INTRINSIC VALUE

Undoubtedly, "bitcoin has no intrinsic value" is one of the phrases most used by its critics. They use this statement as an argument to claim that "bitcoin has no utility", "bitcoin is a purely speculative asset", "bitcoin's price should be 0", "bitcoin cannot function as money", "bitcoin should not be invested in", "bitcoin is a bubble" or that "bitcoin is a fraud". In truth, the sentence with which this paragraph begins is just the starting point for many other arguments against bitcoin.

JPMorgan CEO: Bitcoin Has No Intrinsic Value, Regulators Will 'Regulate the Hell out of It'

Illustration 1: Words by Jamie Dimon, CEO of JPMorgan and one of the most visible critics of Bitcoin. Source: Bitcoin.com.

But before evaluating whether this statement is true or false, and whether that is good or bad, it is important to understand what the term "intrinsic value" means.

According to the Investopedia website:

> *Intrinsic value is a measure of what an asset is worth. This measure is arrived at by means of an objective calculation or complex financial model. Intrinsic value is different from the current market price of an asset. [...] Financial analysis uses cash flow to determine the intrinsic, or underlying, value of a company or stock.*

(Investopedia, 2022)

In the financial world, a widely accepted definition is often used that indicates that the intrinsic value of a company is determined by the cash flows it generates. Therefore, some critics who are familiar with the world of traditional finance claim that Bitcoin has no intrinsic value because it does not generate cash flows. If we stick to this definition, it is true that bitcoin has no intrinsic value. However, comparing Bitcoin to a company is a mistake.

Bitcoin is a decentralized system that is not controlled by one or more people and does not pay dividends to its holders. But saying that Bitcoin has no value for this reason is a clear indicator of not understanding what Bitcoin is, why it was created and what its purpose is. Bitcoin was born as a protocol for the transmission of value without intermediaries, and the unit of value used in the network is bitcoin, a new form of money through and for the Internet, in which transmitting value is as easy as sending an email.

The value of money

Throughout history there have been many forms of money: seashells, salt, precious stones, gold, central bank money, and we could go on. None of them has generated cash flows and despite this, we obviously give them value. What is the value of an asset that aspires to become a generalized form of money based on? Its value is determined by how it fulfills the three main functions of money: medium of exchange, store of value, and unit of account. That is, the value of a certain form of money is what makes it work well as money, solely and exclusively. It doesn't need to have other utilities.

Some will argue that gold, which functioned as money for more than 5,000 years and currently continues to function as a store of value, does have intrinsic value beyond its value as money, since it is used for other purposes: jewelry, electronics, etc. Despite being true, the percentage of gold that is used for said purposes compared to what is used as a store of value is practically negligible. And it is this function as a store of value that mainly affects its price in the market. If people suddenly decided that they no longer want to use it as a store of value and all this gold was sold, its price would drop dramatically. But we could even say that the fact that money has other uses can be counterproductive. If an incredibly important utility were discovered for such an asset that functions as money, what could happen is that people stop using it as a form of exchange or savings and end up losing its function as money.

Its functions as a medium of exchange, store of value, or unit of account give bitcoin value. But is that its intrinsic value? When speaking of an intrinsic quality, we normally refer to an innate property and not born as a source of a need. In moral philosophy, a distinction is made between intrinsic value and extrinsic or instrumental value depending on whether something has value by itself or if it is obtained as a means to achieve an end, respectively. A tool or appliance, such as a hammer or washing machine, has instrumental value because it helps drive a nail or clean clothes. Happiness and pleasure are generally considered to have intrinsic value to the extent that asking why someone would want them makes little sense: they are desirable in themselves, independent of their possible instrumental value.

Ludwig von Mises, a renowned Austrian historian, philosopher, and economist, said:

> *Value is not intrinsic, it is not in things. It is within us; it is the way in which man reacts to the conditions of his environment. Neither is value in words and doctrines, it is reflected in human conduct. It is not what a man or groups of men say about value that counts, but how they act.*

Money is a human creation whose objective is to provide the three functions that we have previously discussed. Therefore, we can affirm that these functions are its extrinsic value, it is not born with them. What are the properties that allow us to "measure" the instrumental value of something that claims to function as money? Vijay Boyapati (2018) gives us in *The Bullish Case for Bitcoin*(Boyapati, 2018) the list of properties normally accepted as properties that a good must have to function well as money:

1. Durable: it must be non-perishable and resistant. It is for this reason that tomatoes would not be a good store of value. Bitcoin has no physical form, so its durability is determined by the durability of the Bitcoin network. It has been running for a relatively short time and it is too soon to say if it will last or not;

however, it is very encouraging given the resistance of this type of P2P networks against attacks or failures.

2.   Transportable: it must be easily stored and transportable. This allows us to take it with us in case we have to move to another part of the world. In this sense, a light asset with little volume will fulfill this property better than a heavy or bulky element. Bitcoin does not take up physical space since it is stored in the nodes of the network. To access my funds I only need to write or memorize a private key, regardless of whether it gives access to 1 bitcoin or 21 million. I can take it anywhere with no effort.

3.   Fungible: it is desirable that any unit of a good that functions as money is interchangeable for other units of this good, making it impossible to distinguish between some units and others. Without fungibility, the problem of coincidence of desires increases and privacy in exchanges is lost. In this sense, gold works better than seashells, since each shell has a different shape, size, or color. In the case of Bitcoin, today it cannot be considered fungible unless additional mechanisms are used to increase privacy. Every transaction and bitcoin is traceable. If certain bitcoins have passed through an address involved in some illegal activity, they could become "tainted" and not be treated the same as the rest.

4.   Verifiable: it is important that it can be easily verified that said good is authentic and not a counterfeit. Trusting that we are getting something real will make it easier for the exchange to take place. Bitcoins can be verified with mathematical certainty. By using

cryptographic signatures, a bitcoin owner can publicly prove that they own the bitcoins they claim to own.

5.   Divisible: it must be easily divisible into smaller parts. Something that cannot be divided makes it difficult to exchange in large and complex societies, with a greater number of goods that can be exchanged with each other. Bitcoins can be divided and transmitted up to one hundred millionth of a bitcoin (satoshis).

6.   Scarce: it is desirable that the good does not exist in abundance or be easy to obtain or produce. Scarcity is perhaps the most relevant attribute of a store of value, as it taps into the innate human desire to collect what is rare. It is the source of the original value of the store of value. An uncontrolled increase in supply generates a devaluation of said good. Bitcoin is the big winner in this category. It is written in the code that no more of 21 million will ever exist, 19 of which have already been created. This gives the bitcoin owner a known percentage of the total possible supply and the assurance that the percentage of the total will never change.

7.   History Established: the longer society perceives the good to have been valuable, the greater its attractiveness as a store of value. A long-established store of value will be difficult to displace for a different good, except by force or if the new good has a significant advantage among the other attributes listed above. Bitcoin, despite its short existence, has passed enough tests in the market for it to be gone in no time. The Lindy effect suggests that the longer Bitcoin exists, the greater society's confidence that it will continue to exist

in the future.

8.   Censorship resistant: a new attribute, which has become increasingly important in our modern digital society, is censorship resistance. That is, how difficult is it for a third party such as a corporation or a state to prevent the owner of the property from keeping and using it. Censorship resistant goods are ideal for those living under regimes trying to impose capital controls or prohibit various forms of peaceful commerce. In the transmission of bitcoins there is no human intervention in deciding whether or not to allow the. As a distributed peer-to-peer network, Bitcoin is, by its very nature, designed to be resistant to censorship.

These properties give Bitcoin its value and make this new asset the best existing form of money known to man. Do these properties alone have intrinsic value? No. The fact that the number of units of an asset is low is something positive if it is going to be used as a form of money, but it would be considered negative in other circumstances, for example, if we are talking about water or oxygen on Earth. Also, its "intrinsic value" can change over time. The value that we can give to water is different depending on whether it is hot or not, if we have played sports, or if we have not drunk for 2 days and we are about to become dehydrated.

JPMorgan Becomes The First Big Bank To Give Retail Clients Access To Bitcoin

Figure 2: It looks like JPMorgan eventually found value in Bitcoin. 22/July/2021. Source: Nasdaq.com.

Conclusion

We can conclude that, despite the fact that the concept of intrinsic value is attractive and seems correct, in most cases we are talking about instrumental value, subjective to the person, time and place. Bitcoin has extrinsic value and does not bring the same value to everyone at all times. That does not mean that it is not useful, quite the contrary. If I am fleeing from one country to another and want to take all my money with me without being seized, Bitcoin brings me a lot of value, possibly more than in other circumstances. Bitcoin provides great value as money, and money does not need to have any other utility beyond simply functioning as money.

2

BITCOIN IS A FRAUD, A PYRAMID SCHEME, A PONZI

Classifying bitcoin as a fraud is yet another of the repetitive assertions made by both the ignorant and the naysayers. On many occasions, such criticism is based on statements such as "bitcoin has no intrinsic value", "bitcoin has no utility" or "bitcoin is pure speculation".

Is bitcoin really a fraud or a pyramid scheme? Before we can say if there is any truth in this statement, let's see how the CNMV, Spain's securities market regulator, classifies a scam or financial fraud:

> *A financial fraud is an action carried out by a person or company that causes economic damage to a third party by means of deception and for profit.*
>
> (CNMV, 2022)

In the above definition there are two interesting points that we can analyze and compare with bitcoin:

-    It is an action performed by a person or company.

-    Causes economic damage to a third party by means of deception and for profit.

Let's analyze these two points.

A financial fraud is an action carried out by a person or company

Bitcoin is not controlled by one person, company, or entity. Bitcoin was announced to the world on October 31, 2008, when a person or group of people under the pseudonym Satoshi Nakamoto published the white paper in an academic-format article describing how it works. Two months later, Nakamoto would launch the network and make the code public so that anyone could join the network and participate in the development of the protocol. Nakamoto continued to collaborate on the project until 2011, the year in which it vanished.

Despite numerous efforts to find out the identity of the creator of Bitcoin, it remains a mystery. On many occasions, their anonymity is considered as something negative. Why did he prefer to remain anonymous? To avoid consequences if his fraud is discovered? Could it be because he was aware that what he was doing was deeply subversive and that he would become an enemy of the state if Bitcoin succeeded? Or maybe he thought it was vital to a project whose goal was to remain completely decentralized and without a prominent figure or leader?

Today it is considered that he did the right thing in this regard. A person or leader with a certain amount of power in this type of project is still an easily attackable weak point. This is something that had been evident after several previous attempts to create private money in previous decades.

In Bitcoin there are no entities with privileges, with special roles, or with sufficient influence to tip the project towards their interests. The "war" over the block size change between 2015 and 2017 is proof of this. I encourage you to investigate what happened.

A financial fraud causes economic damage to a third party by means of deception and for profit.

Bitcoin itself does not cause financial harm to anyone. Bitcoin is neutral and anyone is free to use the Bitcoin network to transfer, pay or save in the network's native currency, bitcoin. Many people decide to hoard bitcoins, using it as a store of value, with the aim of not losing purchasing power in an economic framework of galloping inflation and distrust in central banks.

Is there fraud around bitcoin? Yes of course. Just like there are in any other sector, be it financial, real estate, services, etc. Bitcoin, the protocol, should not be confused with malicious actors who use it for illegal or fraudulent purposes. It would be like saying that the

Internet is a fraud because it is used to commit crimes and fraud.

After analyzing these two points, it seems clear that bitcoin does not fit the definition of fraud. But "fraud" is too general a concept. Let's turn to the specific case of frauds known as pyramid schemes and Ponzi schemes.

In economics, a **pyramid scheme** refers to a business scheme in which participants must recommend and attract (refer) more clients with the objective of generating profits for the original participants. It is required that the number of new participants be greater than the number of existing ones, hence the name pyramid.

Ponzi schemes are a type of pyramid scheme in which an individual or organization operates as the head of the pyramid but presents themselves as an investment broker. The pyramid owner receives contributions from participants who promise to invest again and receive their initial investment along with exceptionally high interest. However, such investments do not exist, and instead, the contributions from the latest participants are used to pay off those who entered earlier.

Illustration 3: Representation of a pyramid scheme.

Characteristics of a pyramid scheme

Pyramid schemes have a number of common characteristics:

1. Promise of benefit

Whereas, in pyramid schemes, the fraud promoter promises high returns with "no risk", in bitcoin there is no promise of profit. Nakamoto never promised investment returns, let alone high or consistent investment returns.

Nakamoto practically never talked about financial gains. He wrote mainly about technical aspects, about freedom, about the problems of the modern banking system and so on. He wrote mainly as a programmer, occasionally as an economist, and never as a marketer.

Bitcoins have no dividend or potential future dividend, therefore not like a stock. More like a collectible or commodity.

(Nakamoto, Re: Bitcoins are most like shares of common stock, 2010)

Some people decide to invest in bitcoin with the objective of later selling it for a profit. Does this make it a Ponzi? If someone buys bitcoin in the hope of selling it at a higher price than the purchase, it is no different from investing in gold, currencies, fixed income, equities, or concert tickets with the aim of reselling them. Investors (and speculators), as a rule, always invest with the hope that what they are buying will increase in value, whether in the short, medium, or long term.

There are and will be predictions about its future price. We must be cautious and listen to such predictions with skepticism or at least question them before being swayed by the advice of third parties.

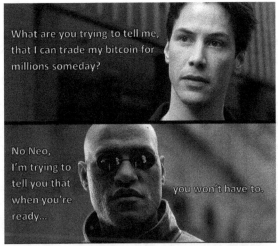

Illustration 4: Popular meme of bitcoin and Matrix meme.

Whether the value and price of bitcoin will increase will depend on its adoption as money and its utility. Greater usage will likely mean greater capitalization to meet demand. While in the case of traditional currencies their capitalization normally increases as the number of units increases, Bitcoin chooses to make the creation of new currencies predictable and limit their quantity over time, which in theory will lead to an increase in value if the demand exceeds supply.

> *The fact that new coins are produced means the money supply increases by a planned amount, but this does not necessarily result in inflation. If the supply of money increases at the same rate that the number of people using it increases, prices remain stable. If it does not increase as fast as demand, there will be deflation and early holders of money will see its value increase.*

(Nakamoto, Bitcoin P2P e-cash paper, 2008)

2. Lack of transparency

Typically, pyramid schemes and Ponzi schemes hide information or outright lie to participants about what their money is used for or where the promised economic benefit comes from. In other words, Ponzi schemes base their model largely on concealment and deception.

Bitcoin, in the other hand, is completely public and transparent. Its code has been accessible to everyone from the very beginning, and can be downloaded and run by anyone who wants to, whenever they want to.

> *Being open source means anyone can independently review the code. If it was closed source, nobody could verify the security. I think it's essential for a program of this nature to be open source.*

(Nakamoto, Re: Questions about Bitcoin, 2009)

The Bitcoin code describes how it works, including how it is created and distributed. The monetary policy of coin creation and its distribution is also transparent and predictable. People who participate in the network by running the Bitcoin code are free to stop doing so at any time if they disagree with the decisions made about the future of the network.

```
CAmount GetBlockSubsidy(int nHeight, const Consensus::Params& consensusParams)
{
    int halvings = nHeight / consensusParams.nSubsidyHalvingInterval;
    // Force block reward to zero when right shift is undefined.
    if (halvings >= 64)
        return 0;

    CAmount nSubsidy = 50 * COIN;
    // Subsidy is cut in half every 210,000 blocks which will occur
    // approximately every 4 years.
    nSubsidy >>= halvings;
    return nSubsidy;
}
```

Illustration 5: Code with the distribution of new bitcoins (subsidy).

3. Need to attract new investors

A Ponzi scheme requires a continuous flow of new investors to pay existing investors. The Bitcoin protocol is oblivious to the price at which bitcoin is bought or sold and does not require new investors to maintain its value in terms of utility. Even if its price fell to zero, the network would continue to function as it has so far. All it needs is at least one person running the Bitcoin code, a node.

It is important to note that bitcoin was not priced in dollars until almost a year after its launch, when the first P2P trading platform, New Liberty Standard, was created. Not having a dollar price did not stop people from attaching value to it and expending energy to mine, collect and transfer it.

> *During 2009 my exchange rate was calculated by dividing $1.00 by the average amount of electricity required to run a computer with high CPU for a year, 1331.5 kWh, multiplied by the average residential cost of electricity in the United States for the previous year, $0.1136, divided by 12 months divided by the number*

of bitcoins generated by my computer over the past 30 days.

(NewLibertyStandard, 2009)

If Satoshi Nakamoto had launched Bitcoin as a form of pyramid scheme, he would probably by now have sold at least part of the million bitcoins he allegedly mined during his involvement with the project. Nakamoto mined these bitcoins in the same way as everyone else, bringing computational power and the corresponding security to the network. Today, he has not moved a single bitcoin, beyond those that he exchanged with other collaborators in the project such as Hal Finney.

Conclusion

Bitcoin does not fit the definition of fraud or pyramid scheme. It has utility as currency, and its value will remain as long as people continue to find value in its utility. Bitcoin is not controlled by one entity or group of people, is completely transparent, promises no financial benefits to those who invest or own it, and does not require new investors to keep it going.

3

BITCOIN WASTES ENERGY

This is possibly the most controversial criticism and the one that has been analyzed the most with more or less serious studies both for and against. It is also one of the most subjective points and one that will hardly tip the balance to one side or the other. It is difficult to put a limit on how much energy is "enough".

The questions we must ask ourselves are, then: Does the Bitcoin network represent an unnecessary waste of energy? Can the same objective and result be achieved without this energy consumption? Is Bitcoin bad for the environment?

In order to answer these questions, it is first necessary to understand how and for what purpose Bitcoin consumes said energy.

Mining, Proof of Work and Decentralized Consensus

You may have heard the term "bitcoin mining", "mining nodes" or "mining farms" when talking about Bitcoin. And you may have heard that it is those miners and mining farms that are responsible for that "waste" of energy. What is this mining thing and why is it needed?

Generally, when talking about mining on the Bitcoin network, reference is made to one of its main functions: the creation and distribution of new bitcoins. With each block of transactions that is created in Bitcoin, new coins are minted and given as a reward to the miner who proposed the new block. This mechanism sets monetary policy in Bitcoin.

> *By convention, the first transaction in a block is a special transaction that starts a new coin owned by the creator of the block. This adds an incentive for nodes to support the network, and provides a way to initially distribute coins into circulation, since there is no central authority to issue them. The steady addition of a constant of amount of new coins is analogous to gold miners expending resources to add gold to circulation. In our case, it is CPU time and electricity that is expended.*

(Nakamoto, Bitcoin: A Peer-to-Peer Electronic Cash System, 2008)

It is often referred to as mining because the reward (creation of new coins) is designed to simulate diminishing returns, just like mining for precious metals. The number of bitcoins a miner can create with each block is halved every 210,000 blocks (or approximately 4 years). It started with 50 bitcoins per block in January 2009 and was reduced to 25 bitcoins per block in November 2012, to 12.5 bitcoins in July 2016, and again to 6.25 bitcoins in May 2020. Based on this formula, bitcoin mining rewards decrease exponentially until approximately the year 2140, when all bitcoins will have been issued (20.99999999 million).

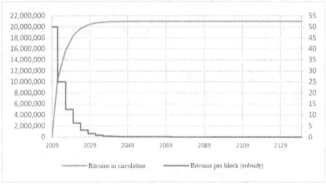

Illustration 6: Growth rate and number of bitcoins in circulation.

For a detailed description of how mining, proof-of-work and decentralized consensus work in Bitcoin you can go to *The Bitcoin Fundamentals*.

The Bitcoin white paper continues with:

> *The incentive may help encourage nodes to stay honest. If a greedy attacker is able to assemble more CPU power than all the honest nodes, he would have to choose between using it to defraud people by stealing back his payments, or using it to generate new coins. He ought to find it more profitable to play by the rules, such rules*

*that favour him with more new coins than everyone else
combined, than to undermine the system and the validity
of his own wealth.*

Although mining is reward-incentivized, the primary purpose of mining is not the generation of new coins. To view mining only as the process by which coins are created is to confuse the means (incentives) with the goal of the process. Nor would it be correct to think that the objective of mining is to validate transactions. This leads to headlines such as the following:

Every Bitcoin transaction – even buying a latte – consumes over \$100 in electricity, says a new report
(Tully, 2021)

Bitcoin has been validating the same number of transactions per second and generating blocks every 10 minutes on average since the beginning, regardless of the fact that power consumption has increased enormously since its launch. The reality is that it is the full nodes and not the miners who validate the transactions and who introduce the new coins by accepting the blocks proposed by the miners.

So, what is the goal of Bitcoin mining? Mining is the invention that makes Bitcoin special, as it is a decentralized security mechanism that is the foundation of P2P digital money. The network could be powered by a single mining node, as it did when only Nakamoto ran the Bitcoin code at the time of its launch, but it would be highly vulnerable to attack. To succeed in the performing a double spend, one must exceed in computational power the aggregate of all nodes acting in good faith in exchange for the rewards. Knowing what we know today, it would be impossible to repeat the launch of Bitcoin as it happened, since it would likely be attacked immediately.

We can then focus the question on whether it is worth the energy consumption to keep a network like Bitcoin secure and decentralized. A decentralized digital monetary system, separate from any sovereign entity, with rule-based monetary policy and inherent scarcity, gives people around the world an option, which some of them use to store value or to transmit that value to others. almost instantly anywhere in the world. Until the creation of Bitcoin, this was impossible. Bitcoin was the culmination of years of study and work by some of the greatest minds in the field of cryptography and computing since the 1970s.

Therefore, to say that the energy needed to maintain the best existing form of money is spent unjustifiably is, to say the least, questionable.

> *It's the same situation as gold and gold mining. The marginal cost of gold mining tends to stay near the price of gold. Gold mining is a waste, but that waste is far less than the utility of having gold available as a medium of exchange.*

> *I think the case will be the same for Bitcoin. The utility of the exchanges made possible by Bitcoin will far exceed the cost of electricity used. Therefore, not having Bitcoin would be the net waste.*

(Nakamoto, Re: Bitcoin minting is
thermodynamically perverse, 2010)

Is it possible to replicate such a system without
spending energy or with a significantly lower cost?

This is a frequent claim among projects that promise to offer an alternative to Bitcoin without sacrificing security or decentralization and even promising a greater scalability. The truth is that, until the creation of Bitcoin, there were many failed attempts. Bitcoin has been running for over thirteen years without major problems.

Mining or proof of work anchors Bitcoin's security model to a tangible "real world" asset, electricity. In this way, the security of the network does not depend on the price of the token itself, as occurs in other decentralized consensus models.

Proof-of-stake or similar models rely on a sufficiently high price of the token itself that it makes it unfeasible for someone to acquire enough tokens. No one can ensure that a state won't "print" money or that its price won't drop enough for someone to get a sufficient percentage to take control of the network. Moreover, if someone manages to take control, it is practically impossible to take it away from them because they will obtain new tokens that allow them to maintain the same percentage. This does not mean that these models will not work, but they are at a very early stage to be able to draw conclusions.

In the case of Bitcoin and proof of work, security depends on someone being able to acquire enough hardware and electrical power to take control of the network, something that seems more complicated being outside the network itself. Also, if this were to happen, anyone could join the network to counter that majority of computing power.

On the other hand, it is currently being discussed which cryptocurrencies are considered commodities, and which are considered securities. Some regulators have already said that only truly decentralized, proof-of-work projects can be considered digital commodities. The usual form of money until the advent of central bank money was known as commodity money or merchandise money.

Can a token be considered a security if by locking it into the consensus algorithm gives a right to future benefits? The answer is unclear, but it is certainly closer to what is considered a security in traditional markets than Bitcoin, which does not give to its holders any rights to the network or future coins minted.

Another common question is whether in the long run different blockchain networks using mining or proof of work will be able to coexist. Despite the fact that there are currently several mining-based networks, the truth is that many have come under attack for not attracting enough computing power for their defense. There are those who argue that the trend will be for only one proof-of-work network to remain and, should that happen, today it seems that Bitcoin has the highest probability of being the "chosen one".

According to Michael Saylor (Saylor, 2022), Bitcoin today represents 99% of all the hashrate in the ecosystem and offers a level of security 100 times higher than the rest of the blockchain networks combined.

What is the limit between acceptable energy consumption and waste? This is another difficult question to answer and one that will never convince everyone. It is evident that Bitcoin consumes a large amount of energy. To assess whether it is justified, it is important to understand the value of Bitcoin. Bitcoin uses energy to provide an alternative, borderless, decentralized, and uncensorable form of money.

Generally speaking, something is considered useful to the extent that it adds value to society. Its energy consumption ceases to be questioned in terms of morality and begins to be seen as an essential human need. The following graph illustrates similar comparisons with other socially accepted utilities despite their energy consumption.

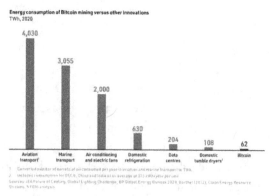

Illustration 7: Why the debate about crypto's energy consumption is flawed. World Economic Forum. March 23, 2022.

There hasn't been any moral debate about the energy impact of home refrigeration or dryers because they serve useful functions in our lives. The difference is that Bitcoin has not yet become a socially accepted tool that performs an essential function, at least not for those living in developed countries. Many of those who write and opine on the energy consumed by Bitcoin do so from a privileged position, they are not users of this technology and do not understand its inherent purpose.

It is estimated that there are more than 300 million people worldwide who own bitcoin, and not all of them live in developed countries. In fact, bitcoin adoption is growing at a faster rate in in Africa, South America, or Asia than it is in North America or Europe.

Bitcoin has become as essential to many who live in developing countries as Netflix and air conditioning to those who live in developed countries.

Does energy consumption and mining pose a climate problem for our planet?

Bitcoin adoption worldwide is estimated to reach 1 billion users by the end of 2023. As that number continues to grow and Bitcoin becomes socially accepted as an essential tool for human civilization, the Bitcoin energy consumption debate will be reoriented towards environmental sustainability solutions to which Bitcoin can make a significant contribution.

Contrary to sensationalist headlines, Bitcoin is becoming a crucial part of the development of a carbon neutral energy grid and has made it economically viable to invest, develop and build renewable energy power generation.

According to Microstrategy studies, CO_2 emissions associated with the production of electricity used for mining represents less than 0.08% of global emissions and is the fastest growing industry in the use of clean energy.

> *Bitcoin runs on stranded, excess energy, generated at the edge of the grid, in places where there is no other demand, at times when no one else needs the electricity.... Bitcoin mining is the most efficient, cleanest industrial use of electricity, and is improving its energy efficiency at the fastest rate across any major industry... Approximately $4-5 billion in electricity is used to power & secure a network that is worth $420 billion as of today, and settles $12 billion per day ($4 trillion per year).*

(Major, 2022)

Conclusion

That bitcoin is useful and brings value to millions of people around the world is evident. Data has been presented in the analysis indicating that energy consumption allows Bitcoin to remain secure and decentralized and that it is lower than that of many industries that could be assumed to be more superfluous and expendable. Even so, as I indicated at the beginning, this is the criticism and analysis that is most subjective to interpretations. While for some, present and future energy consumption is more than justified (or, rather, needs no justification), for others it never will be, regardless of whether the amount of energy is little or much.

4

BITCOIN IS SLOW AND DOES NOT SCALE

Bitcoin can process between 3 and 4 transactions on average per second today, which is equivalent to around 300,000 transactions per day.

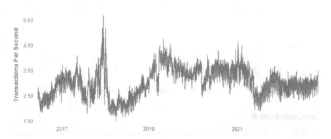

Illustration 8: Graph of transactions per second added to the mempool. Source: blockchain.com.

By comparison, payment networks like Visa can process around 40,000 transactions per second, which is around 10,000 times more than Bitcoin. Also, Bitcoin transactions can take 10 minutes or more to confirm, which has led to it being called "slow". Based on these numbers alone, the qualifier seems justified. In fact, the first response Satoshi Nakamoto got after the publication of the Bitcoin white paper was from James Donald (Donald, 2008), who literally said, "It doesn't seem to scale."

> *We very, very much need such a system, but the way I understand your proposal, it does not seem to scale to the required size.*
>
> *(…)*
>
> *To detect and reject a double spending event in a timely manner, one must have most past transactions of the coins in the transaction, which, naively implemented, requires each peer to have most past transactions, or most past transactions that occurred recently. If hundreds of millions of people are doing transactions, that is a lot of bandwidth - each must know all, or a substantial part thereof.*

In any transactional system, security, decentralization, and speed must be balanced. You can't maximize all of them at the same time. Visa, for example, maximizes speed and offers moderate security at the expense of decentralization. On the other hand, Bitcoin maximizes security and decentralization at the expense of speed.

The limitation on the number of transactions in Bitcoin is determined by:

- Block size. Following the inclusion of SegWit in the Bitcoin protocol, transaction blocks are between 1 and 2 MB in size, or about 2,000 transactions on average per block.

- Block time. The block time is the average duration that elapses between new mined blocks, which in the case of Bitcoin is 10 minutes.

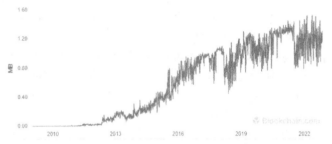

Figure 9: Average block size (MB). Source: blockchain.com.

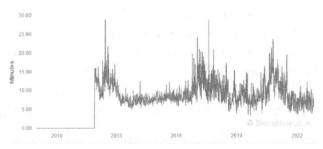

Illustration 10: Average confirmation time. Source: blockchain.com.

Although there have been heated debates within the Bitcoin community about whether to increase the block size or reduce block times to increase the number of transactions per second, no consensus has been reached. In fact, this disagreement led to a hard fork in which the new Bitcoin Cash chain emerged, which decided to increase the block size indefinitely.

Scaling solely by increasing the size of the blocks or reducing the time between blocks leads to network centralization, since only a few users or entities would be able to run the software, given the high demand on hardware and bandwidth requirements.

Perhaps viewing the Bitcoin network as a payment network for day-to-day transactions is not the most appropriate choice, given the cost and time required to confirm transactions. Instead, we should see Bitcoin as a highly secure settlement layer that allows a scarce commodity to be transmitted between accounts, a sort of vault that opens every 10 minutes to update a list of balances.

This makes the comparison between Bitcoin and Visa inappropriate; Visa is just one layer in the financial system that relies on lower settlement layers, with commercial banks and other systems involved below the surface. Consumers may use payment systems such as Visa, Mastercard or PayPal to carry out a large number of small transactions, and the underlying banks settle each other with larger and less frequent transactions. With each layer we go down, security is increased at the cost of reducing its speed. In truth, the payments that we feel as immediate sometimes take more than a week to be confirmed, as they have to settle at the lower layers.

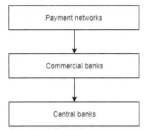

Illustration 11: Multi-layer payment system.

Is it true then that Bitcoin cannot scale? Are there alternatives? And if there are alternatives, what is the way to scale? The answer is simple: by layers, in the same way as in traditional financial systems.

Introducing the Lightning Network

In January 2016, Joseph Poon and Thaddeus Dryja proposed a possible solution to Bitcoin's scalability problem with the publication of *The Bitcoin Lightning Network: Scalable Off-Chain Instant Payments* (Poon & Dryja, 2016).

The Lightning Network proposes a new network, a "second layer", where users can make payments to each other on a peer-to-peer network, without the need to publish each transaction on the Bitcoin block-chain. Users can pay each other on the Lightning Network as many times as they want, without creating additional Bitcoin transactions or incurring fees on the main chain. They only make use of the Bitcoin block-chain to initially "deposit" bitcoins on the Lightning network and to represent the final state, "removing" the bitcoins from the Lightning Network. The result is that many more Bitcoin payments can be made off-chain, with only the initial deposit and final settlement transactions needing to be validated and stored by Bitcoin nodes.

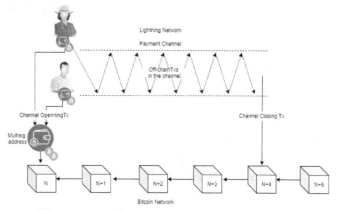

Illustration 12: Bitcoin and Lightning Network layers.

Lightning Network, or LN, is a decentralized peer-to-peer network that uses what are known as *payment channels* implemented as s*mart contracts* (programs deployed in a blockchain network) on the Bitcoin network. LN also defines the protocol that establishes how participants create and execute these smart contracts.

The Lightning Network relies on the Bitcoin network. By using real Bitcoin transactions and its native *scripting* language to create smart contracts, it is possible to create a secure network of participants that can conduct transactions in an almost immediate, secure, and decentralized manner.

> Note: You can find more details about the Lightning network and how it works in *Bitcoin Fundamentals*.

Conclusion

If we limit ourselves to the Bitcoin network, it is true that its speed and cost make it impractical for daily use by the billions of users around the world. However, any blockchain network, not just Bitcoin, will always be slower than a centralized network if it is to retain the properties that make it meaningful: decentralization, security, and censorship resistance.

That said, there are alternatives like the Lightning Network, which is a layer two solution, allowing Bitcoin to scale and offer the ability to send and receive bitcoins instantly and at virtually zero cost. Lightning transactions are Bitcoin transactions that remain off-chain until you want to settle the final state on the Bitcoin network.

5

CRIMINALS USE BITCOIN

"Criminals use bitcoin" or "bitcoin is used for illegal activities" is also one of the most common criticisms. Before looking at such claims, it's important to be honest. Has bitcoin been used for illegal purposes? Yes, without a doubt. Bitcoin has been used as a tool for extortion, financing terrorism, money laundering, acquiring illegal products, among others.

Chanalysis, a company dedicated to the analysis of data from blockchain networks, published in 2022 a report on the use of Bitcoin and other cryptocurrencies for illegal activities (Chainanalysis, 2022). According to said report, cryptocurrency-based crime reached a new all-time high in 2021, with a 79% over the previous year. The value received in cryptocurrencies by addresses involved in illicit activities increased from 7.8 billion in 2020 to 14 billion in 2021.

DEBUNKING COMMON BITCOIN CRITICISMS

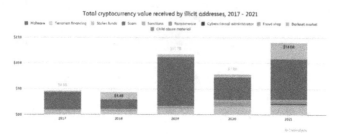

Illustration 13: Value received by addresses involved in illegal activities, 2017-2021. Source: Crypto Crime Trends for 2022. Chainanalysis.

Of course, there is no denying that it is worrying that $14 billion worth of bitcoin and other cryptocurrencies have been used for illicit activities. Does this mean that bitcoin is used only for illegal purposes or in its vast majority? No.

The report goes on to state that not only did illicit use increase, but the total volume transacted in 2021 also increased to $15.8 trillion, an increase of 567% compared to 2020. Not surprisingly, if its overall user increases, do does its use for illegal activities. What is surprising is that the increase in the total volume transacted is almost an order of magnitude higher than the increase in its use in criminal activities.

With these numbers, it can be estimated that the percentage of bitcoin and other cryptocurrencies destined for illegal activities has decreased from 0.62% in 2020 to 0.15% in 2021 of the total transacted.

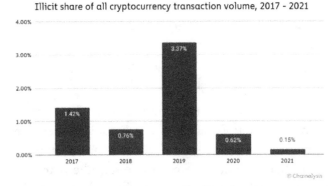

Illustration 14: Percentage of the total volume transacted used for illegal purposes, 2017-2021. Source: Crypto Crime Trends for 2022. Chainanalysis.

How does this leave bitcoin against the dollar or the euro?

It is estimated that in 2020 the world money supply in circulation was of the order of 100 trillion dollars.

Illustration 15: Comparison between markets by capitalization. Source: inbitcoinwetrust.com

The United Nations Office on Drugs and Crime es-
timates that every year up to $2 trillion is laundered
worldwide, that is, at least 2% of the world's money
supply is used for money laundering (European Union
Agency for Criminal Justice Cooperation, 2022).

Worst of all, this estimate only takes into account
money laundering and does not consider other illegal
activities such as the sale of weapons or drugs, for example. Therefore, we can assume that the percentage
of the world's money supply in circulation used for illicit purposes must be much higher than that 2%, a
percentage much higher than that estimated in the case
of bitcoin.

Bitcoin is not used for illicit purposes to a greater
extent than the dollar and possibly any other traditional
currency.

Bitcoin as a tool for good

Bitcoin is used for illicit purposes. The reality is that
money is used for both legal and illegal purposes. It's a
shame, but it is what it is. Bitcoin is a tool that can be
used for good or evil, just like any other tool. However,
focusing on the bad distracts attention from the fun-
damental issue and its consequence. If bitcoin can
work for a criminal, it can work for anyone, and for
bitcoin to be viable as a currency, it must work for everyone, including criminals.

As previously stated, only 0.15% of the total volume
transacted in bitcoin has illicit objectives. What

happens with the other 99.85%? What is it used for? Does this "positive" use justify the other "negative" 0.15%?

What makes bitcoin attractive to criminals is precisely what makes it interesting and useful for the billions of potential users around the world: censorship resistance, pseudonymity, portability, scarcity, neutrality, independence from any centralized entity, instantaneousness, etc. These properties allow everyone to find in bitcoin what they need given their own circumstances, be it as a saving tool, a payment tool, an investment tool, etc. And the truth is that there are already millions of people in the world who use bitcoin legally.

In June 2022, 21 human rights advocates from around the world wrote a letter (Aderinokun et al., 2022) to the US Congress in defense of responsible regulation of bitcoin and cryptocurrencies. The letter responded to a previous "anti-bitcoin" letter from a group of critics who claimed that the usefulness of bitcoin and cryptocurrencies was "unproven" and that it was a solution "looking for a problem". The 21 signatories stated that the majority of the authors of the "anti-bitcoin" letter came from financially privileged countries and that lived a very different reality from the rest of the world population.

As Alex Gladstein, Director of Strategy at the Human Rights Foundation and one of the signatories to the letter, pointed out in his article *Check your Financial Privilege* "only 13% of the world's population is born in countries with stable and reliable currencies"

(Gladstein, 2022). Therefore, assessing whether bitcoin is useful or not only based on the opinion of a small group of people belonging to that 13% would be misleading. Bitcoin has the potential to improve the lives of people around the world, including those who do not have access to stable financial systems or a reliable currency.

As the activists said in their letter, both they and tens of millions of users in countries under authoritarian regimes and unstable economies use Bitcoin today for a variety of purposes that have as a common factor the defense of freedom and human rights:

> *Bitcoin provides financial inclusion and empowerment because it is open and permissionless. Anyone on earth can use it. Bitcoin and stablecoins offer unparalleled access to the global economy for people in countries like Nigeria, Turkey, or Argentina, where local currencies are collapsing, broken, or cut off from the outside world. […]*

> *We can personally attest — as do the enclosed reports from top global media outlets — that when currency catastrophes struck Cuba, Afghanistan, and Venezuela, Bitcoin gave our compatriots refuge. When crackdowns on civil liberties befell Nigeria, Belarus, and Hong Kong, Bitcoin helped keep the fight against authoritarianism afloat. After Russia invaded Ukraine, these technologies (which the critics allege are "not built for purpose") played a role in sustaining democratic resistance — especially in the first few days, when legacy financial systems faltered.*

They closed the letter by calling for responsible regulation that does not limit the use that they already make of Bitcoin today.

Conclusion

Fiat money has failed many people around the world. Whether due to demonetization, inaccessibility, exclusivity, or use as a political weapon, traditional currencies do not serve everyone equally and give privileges to a lucky few.

At this point, Bitcoin no longer needs to prove its usefulness. Since its birth, it has helped millions of people to fight against authoritarianism, slavery, or discrimination. Bitcoin is money that empowers freedom. A money that requires no permissions, has no borders, and is unstoppable.

Bitcoin has the potential to make a real difference for all the people in the world, but especially for the 4 billion people who cannot trust their rulers or who cannot access the banking system. For them, Bitcoin can be a way out.

I would like to end this chapter with a few words from Andreas Antonopoulos included in his book Internet of Money (Antonopulos, 2017):

> *This is why bitcoin is important to me.*
>
> *Approximately 1 billion people currently have access to banking, credit, and international finance capabilities—primarily the upper classes, the Western nations.*

Six and a half billion people on this planet have no connection to the world of money. They operate in cash-based societies with very little access to international resources. They don't need banks. Two billion of these people are already on the internet. With a simple application download, they can immediately become participants in an international economy, using an international currency that can be transmitted anywhere with no fees and no government controls. They can connect to a world of international finance that is completely peer-to-peer. Bitcoin is the money of the people. At its center are simple mathematical rules that everyone agrees on and no one controls. The possibility of connecting these 6 1/2 billion people to the rest of the world is truly revolutionary.

6

BITCOIN WILL BE REPLACED

Since the invention of Bitcoin, other digital assets have appeared that claim to "fix" Bitcoin's shortcomings. Either because they are faster, more decentralized, more secure, cleaner, allow a higher number of transactions per second, have less volatility, among other features. Although some of these statements may or may not be true in specific cases, what is not so easy to understand is that the value of Bitcoin is not only due to one or more of these properties.

While the Bitcoin software is open source and can be forked and "improved", its **network effect** and broad stakeholder group (users, miners, validators, developers, service providers) make this network valuable in a way that other networks are not and that it is not so easily achieved. Network effects have huge implications for Bitcoin's usefulness as a medium of exchange and store of value. Like any form of money, Bitcoin's value depends on whether someone is willing to accept it as payment, use it as a form of saving mechanism, or use it as a form of investment.

Carl Menger, father of the Austrian school of economics and founder of marginal analysis in economics, calls "saleability" the ease with which a product or good can be sold on the market whenever its owner wishes, with the least detriment to its price. The relative saleability of a product can be assessed based on how well it addresses all three facets of the want mismatch problem: its salability across scales, across space, and across time.

Metcalfe's Law, first formulated in 1976 by Robert Metcalfe in connection with Ethernet, explains the network effects of communication technologies and networks, such as the Internet or the World Wide Web. The law tells us that the value of a telecommunications network increases proportionally to the square of the number of users in the system (n^2) and is often illustrated with the example of a telephone network: a single telephone is useless, but its value increases with the total number of phones in the network, because the number of people you can communicate with increases.

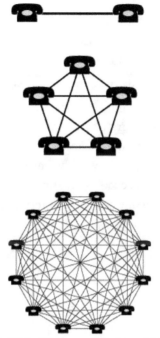

Illustration 16: Metcalfe's Law applied to a telephone network.

The network effect in monetary networks is no different, on the contrary, it has a greater importance. If people are looking for a digital asset as a monetary good, one with the ability to act as a store of value, then they will typically choose the one with the largest, most secure, most decentralized, and most liquid network.

Bitcoin is not MySpace

Sometimes the comparison of Bitcoin with MySpace is also used. MySpace was one of the first social networks and the most used worldwide between 2005 and 2008, the year in which it was surpassed by Facebook and in which its decline began. Could another cryptocurrency appear to replace Bitcoin?

The first mistake here is to consider that Bitcoin is the first form of digital money. Bitcoin is the culmination of over 40 years of research, developments, mistakes, and improvements on previous attempts. Before Bitcoin there were many other failed attempts. Bitcoin was the first to succeed in creating a completely decentralized form of money. No, Bitcoin is not MySpace, Bitcoin is Facebook.

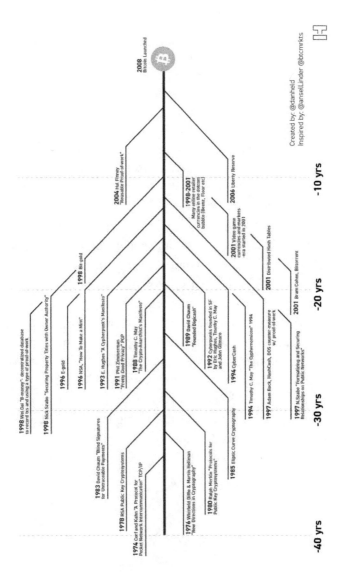

Illustration 17: Developments until the invention of Bitcoin. Source:
https://www.danheld.com/blog/2019/1/6/planting-bitcoinsoil-34

In a recent analysis by Fidelity (Fidelity Digital Assets, 2022), one of the world's largest pension fund and asset managers, the following was said:

> *Bitcoin is fundamentally different from any other digital asset. No other digital asset is likely to improve upon bitcoin as a monetary good because bitcoin is the most (relative to other digital assets) secure, decentralized, sound digital money and any "improvement" will necessarily face tradeoffs.*

With "sacrifices" it meant penalizing certain properties of a network when wanting to improve other properties. This is what is known as the blockchain trilemma and which explains that the properties of a network of this type, such as decentralization, security, and scalability, are interrelated and any improvement in one of them implies a sacrifice in the other two. Bitcoin users value decentralization and security over scalability, which allows it to work well as a store of value. To improve its scalability, higher layer solutions, such as the Lightning Network, are bien pursued.

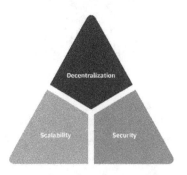

Illustration 18: Triangle representing the blockchain trilemma and the 3 constraints: scalability, security, and decentralization.

Bitcoin is the way it is after thoughtful decisions and years of effort and dedication. It is not the result of random decisions or on a whim.

Conclusion

The network effect has huge implications for the utility of a currency. Adoption of a network is more difficult at first and becomes progressively easier with each new person who starts using it.

This powerful phenomenon favors whichever product has the largest user base, regardless of the product's underlying utility. This means that currencies that are well established with large user bases have strong lock-in effects, which incentivizes people to keep using them.

Bitcoin adoption has increased steadily since its inception in 2009. Each new user makes it more attractive for the next person to join the network. Bitcoin has passed the initial and more complicated phases for a network of this type. It is in this phase that it was especially vulnerable and easier to be attacked.

Bitcoin already exists as an option, and its monetary properties become stronger over time. This is fundamentally why emerging properties in bitcoin are nearly impossible to replicate and overcome.

As is sometimes said, for a new network to replace one that is already established and used by the majority, it is not enough to be a little better, but rather it must be 10 times better. Something that, at least until now, has not occurred and that seems difficult given the restrictions of the blockchain trilemma that we talked about before. Can it happen at some point? Although the possibility that another cryptocurrency could overtake Bitcoin in the future cannot be ruled out, it seems unlikely at present.

7

BITCOIN'S SECURITY MODEL IS UNSUSTAINABLE

Every 10 minutes on average, a new block is created on the Bitcoin network. This block includes a list of transactions that are processed in that block, along with the fee paid for each of these transactions, and a special transaction called *coinbase* that adds new bitcoins to the network. These new bitcoins are called "subsidy". The sum of the transaction fee plus the new bitcoins issued represents the reward for the mining node that created the block.

Based on the monetary policy programmed into the Bitcoin code, the number of bitcoins generated in each block decreases over time. It started with 50 bitcoins per block and this number halves every 210,000 blocks, which is equivalent to approximately four years. With simple mathematical calculations, it is concluded that the total number of bitcoins will be 21 million and the

last fraction of bitcoin will be created around the year
2140.

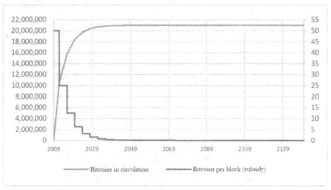

Figure 19: Bitcoin creation rate per block and number of bitcoins in circulation.

Why is this so important and what does it have to
do with Bitcoin security? Bitcoin mining is a competition between the mining nodes to find the solution to
the proof of work. These nodes contribute computational power, which becomes a defense mechanism
against malicious actors, and in return, the network rewards them with an incentive system. This is known as
game theory and is how it is applied in the Bitcoin network.

In 2023, miners will be rewarded with approximately 300,000 bitcoins. At an average bitcoin price of
€25,000, the total amount of rewards for mines would
be approximately €8.25 billion, to which transaction
fees would be added. This is an estimate and the exact
figure will not be known until the end of the year.

The following graph shows the rewards paid to miners, also known as the "security budget", in relation to the market capitalization of bitcoin:

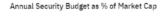

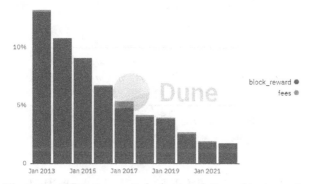

Illustration 20Bitcoin security budget in relation to bitcoin market capitalization. Source: https://dune.com/niftytable/bitcoin-security-budget

As bitcoin's market capitalization has increased, so has the absolute amount spent on security, although the percentage in relation to bitcoin's market capitalization allocate for this purpose has decreased. This trend is expected and foreseeable. At first, it was necessary to spend a large percentage of the market capitalization on security due to the small scale, high vulnerability, and high inflation of the protocol. However, as the size of the market has become larger and the issuance rate of bitcoins has decreased, 0.5% - 1.5% of the market capitalization spent on security is likely to be sufficient.

After the next halving scheduled for 2024, when bitcoin's issuance rate will be reduced from 6.25 to

3.125 new bitcoins per block created, bitcoin's annual inflation rate will be less than 1% and will continue to decline every 4 years towards zero. To maintain a constant security budget between 0.5% and 1.5% of market capitalization, most of the rewards for miners will have to come from transaction fees.

> *In a few decades when the reward gets too small, the transaction fee will become the main compensation for nodes.*
>
> (Nakamoto, Re: What's with this odd generation?, 2010)

Not without reason, there are those who are concerned that transaction fees alone, or with very small subsidies, will not provide adequate compensation for miners and will end up making the security of the network compromised and Bitcoin vulnerable to attacks.

Due to this concern, some argue that Bitcoin's current model is not sustainable and that a change in the monetary policy and the limited supply of 21 million may be necessary to maintain the security of the network. However, others argue that it is possible that the mass adoption of Bitcoin in the future will increase the demand for transactions and thus fees, which would provide miners with adequate compensation without affecting the security of the network.

Changing monetary policy and the total supply of Bitcoin would entail two things:

1. Question the firmness of bitcoin as a form of money. After all, one of the main functions of money is to act as a store of value. To fulfill this function, it is important to present scarcity through a firm and predictable policy.

2. Dilute the participation of bitcoin holders. Taking this decision would go against the interests of the current holders.

The popular phrase "a bitcoin is a bitcoin" highlights that it is possible to always know what percentage of the total number of bitcoins a user has due to the limitation of 21 million bitcoins, which contrasts with the uncertainty that exists in this regard with any other form of money.

But the code is modifiable, can someone just decide to change it? Of course, anyone can take the code, change it, and run it. It has happened many times throughout the existence of Bitcoin and it will continue to happen. We have the example of Bitcoin Cash, Bitcoin Gold, or Bitcoin Satoshi Vision, among others. For a change to be "accepted" and integrated into the Bitcoin network itself, a consensus is needed from the participants, those who run the program on their computers and who choose which program to run of their own decision. It is they who decide what is Bitcoin and what is not.

But then, if the subsidy model doesn't change and the security model has to be supported by transaction fees, the total paid in fees has to be incredibly high to compensate for the reduction or disappearance of the subsidy, right? That's right, and this can be achieved in two ways that have a very different effect on the network:

1. By keeping the number of transactions per block, also called the block size, constant. In this case, the transaction fee would need to increase proportionally to the security budget. This would mean a considerable increase in fees compared to the current ones.

2. Increasing the number of transactions per block according to the needs. If the budget needs to be increased to keep the network secure, the block size is increased and the fee per transaction is kept constant.

At first glance, the second proposal seems ideal and the clear choice. However, we have already seen in the analysis of the critic "Bitcoin is slow and does not scale" that increasing the block size indefinitely has negative consequences for the decentralization of the network, one of the most important qualities of this type of system that should not be sacrificed. It seems then that the only alternative is for the transaction fees to increase progressively with the security budget. Would that mean that Bitcoin would no longer be viable for people with few resources? How can such a proposal be adapted without representing a barrier for the common user to continue using Bitcoin for relatively small transactions?

We have already seen the answer: the implementation of second layers, such as the Lightning Network. The same solution, which serves to scale the number of transactions that the network can process, serves to maintain a scalable security model.

Transactional density

With layer 2 solutions, each transaction on the Bitcoin network can represent tens, thousands, or millions of transactions at the upper layer that are later aggregated and settled at layer 1. Nic Carter, in *Ten Years of Bitcoin: Evaluating Its Performance as a Monetary System* (Carter, 2019), calls this "transactional density". In this way, the transaction fee in Bitcoin is diluted among all the transactions that are aggregated in the upper layer.

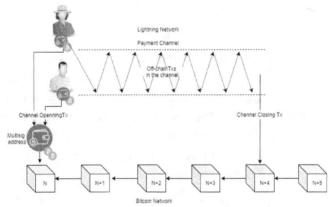

Figure 21: Increase of transactional density through the Lightning Network.

For example, if the average fee per transaction needed to be 0.01 bitcoins to keep the network secure, or approximately €250 at today's exchange rate, that amount would make the use of Bitcoin for low-cost transactions unfeasible. However, if that transaction at layer 1 actually represents 1,000 transactions at layer 2, the actual cost per transaction would be 0.00001, or about €0.25.

Of course, someone could decide to continue using layer 1 to send their individual high-volume transactions, paying that 0.01 bitcoin fee. The model of increasing transactional density is the one that seems most sustainable in the long term, allowing to keep the network secure as its adoption increases and the subsidy is reduced, without posing a risk to the decentralization of the network or an unsustainable increase in fees.

Conclusion

While both the subsidy and transaction fees represent part of Bitcoin's "security budget or expense," their purpose is very different. The subsidy represents a fair way to create and distribute new bitcoins, and a way to boost bitcoin adoption through periodically repeating business cycles or bubbles, giving rise to new waves of speculative buyers that are here to stay.

The subsidy is especially important during the first years of Bitcoin's life, when it is most vulnerable. As the years go by and the subsidy tends to zero, most of the security budget should come from transaction fees. Of the different mechanisms on how to maintain a sustainable security model, it seems that the most reasonable is one in which the fees on the Bitcoin network grow proportionally to maintain a security budget of between 0.5 and 1.5%. % of market capitalization.

So that this does not end up affecting the viability of using the network for small-volume transactions, it is expected that layers on top of Bitcoin such as the Lightning Network or sidechains play a key role, grouping a high number of transactions that are settled together in the Bitcoin network. i.e., thus increasing the transactional density and reducing the fee per individual transaction.

That said, this is just theory, and it's difficult to predict whether the same model will work for the next 10, 50, or 100 years. We will have to see over time if it is necessary to adopt other types of mechanisms that do not compromise the security of the Bitcoin network.

8

BITCOIN WILL BE SHUT DOWN OR BANNED

Another of the most recurring arguments about Bitcoin is that governments will try to shut it down or ban it. Among the reasons and properties of Bitcoin for which they may want this to happen are the following:

- Anonymity: although Bitcoin does not provide complete anonymity, it can offer great privacy if used properly, allowing users to avoid the oversight of the conventional financial system. This makes it difficult for governments to track and monitor the activity of their citizens. It is necessary to remember that privacy is not the same as secrecy or synonymous with doing something bad. Bitcoin exists in large part, thanks to the anonymity of Satoshi Nakamoto.

- Censorship Resistance: Bitcoin transactions are virtually irreversible and impossible to block, meaning that anyone can send bitcoin to anyone else. Compared to the traditional financial system, where accounts can be frozen or emptied unilaterally, Bitcoin represents a challenge for governments.

- Threat to traditional currencies: governments maintain significant control over the population and the economy by forcing their citizens to use a currency that only they can control. Their ability to spend and pay down debt also depends on their ability to print new money. When a superior currency like bitcoin exists, it hinders that ability.

However, it is important to distinguish between shutting down the Bitcoin network and prohibiting or discouraging its use. The former refers to the network ceasing to provide services altogether and being unavailable for use worldwide, while the latter focuses on limiting its use through laws that make it illegal activity or at least discourage its use. discourage. Let's look at each of these scenarios separately.

Bitcoin will be shut down

Bitcoin is a peer-to-peer network designed to run over the Internet. In a P2P network, the nodes that make up the network are the same and there is no centralized hierarchy. The Bitcoin network is constructed with a flat topology, which means there is no central server or centralized service. Instead, the nodes offer and consume services at the same time, which acts as an incentive for their participation.

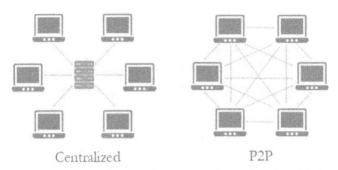

Illustration 22: Centralized architecture Vs. P2P networks.

Bitcoin's P2P network architecture was designed to be resilient and difficult to shut down. Due to its decentralized nature, the Bitcoin network will continue to function as long as there are enough computers running the Bitcoin software and connected to the network. In fact, with only one active node left, the network would continue to function and it would be possible to recover it with new nodes joining the network.

In addition, the Bitcoin network uses a cryptographic protocol called proof of work, which guarantees the security and inviolability of the transactions that are added to the blockchain. This protocol is computationally intensive and requires a large amount of electricity, making it difficult for a single entity to control the network.

Overall, the decentralized and resilient design of the Bitcoin network makes it unlikely that it could be completely shut down from a technical standpoint. Even in a scenario of a complete Internet shutdown, Bitcoin could still function through alternative forms of information communication, such as satellites or radio waves.

But if Bitcoin can't be stopped, can it at least be banned? What effects would such a ban have?

Bitcoin will be banned

Bitcoin has come under fire from government figures, leading to attempts to ban or discourage its use. There are several strategies a government could use to restrict the use of Bitcoin, including:

- Outright ban: a government could outlaw the possession, use, or trade of Bitcoin. However, this would be difficult to implement in practice, as Bitcoin is a global, decentralized network that is difficult to control.

- Transaction restrictions: Instead of outright banning the use of Bitcoin, a government could limit or restrict Bitcoin transactions. For example, it could impose limits on the amount of Bitcoin that can be bought or sold or prohibit certain types of transactions. However, this would also be difficult to implement since Bitcoin allows unrestricted global transactions.

- Taxes and regulations: a government could impose stricter taxes or regulations on Bitcoin transactions, which could discourage its use. For example, it could require businesses that accept Bitcoin to pay additional taxes or require Bitcoin transactions to be reported to tax authorities.

- Information campaigns: a government could launch information campaigns to educate the population about the risks and disadvantages of using Bitcoin. This could make fewer people willing to use Bitcoin due to security concerns or a lack of consumer protection.

However, a government's restrictions and prohibitions can have significant economic and social consequences. Examples such as the ban of owning gold in the United States (1933-1974) and the Prohibition law (1920-1932) show how restrictive measures on the possession or use of certain goods can have unintended effects. If an attempt were made to ban Bitcoin, there could be a number of consequences, including:

- Economic Impact: the ban on owning gold and the Prohibition law had significant economic consequences, such as job losses and the weakening of the economy. If Bitcoin were to be banned, similar negative consequences could follow, such as job losses in the cryptocurrency industry and a decline in investment in Bitcoin-related technologies.

- Criminal Activity: Prohibition law significantly increased alcohol-related criminal activity, while the ban on owning gold created a black market and proliferation of illegal activities. A Bitcoin ban could also lead to Bitcoin-related criminal activity and a black market.

- Effectiveness: the ban on owning gold and the Prohibition law significantly reduced the possession and consumption of the affected goods. However, both measures also led to the creation of illegal activities and black markets. It is difficult to predict whether a Bitcoin ban would be effective, as the decentralized nature of Bitcoin makes it difficult to control.

- Social repercussions: the Prohibition law and the ban on owning gold were perceived as violations of personal liberties. A Bitcoin ban could increase mistrust in the government and financial institutions, and lead to an increase in criminal activity.

As part of the ban on owning gold in 1933, Executive Order 6102 was signed. This rule required United States citizens to hand over to the Federal Reserve all the gold they had, whether in coins, bullions, or certificates, in exchange for receiving $20.67 for each troy ounce (31.1 grams) delivered. Violators of this rule would suffer fines of up to $10,000, ten years in prison, or both penalties at the same time.

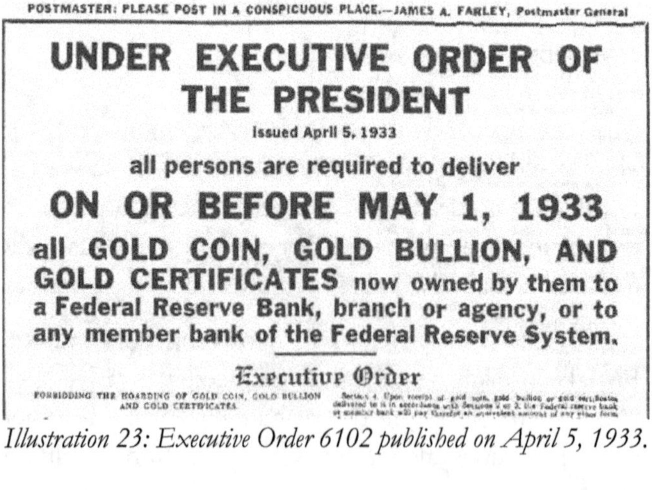

POSTMASTER: PLEASE POST IN A CONSPICUOUS PLACE.—JAMES A. FARLEY, Postmaster General

UNDER EXECUTIVE ORDER OF THE PRESIDENT

Issued April 5, 1933

all persons are required to deliver

ON OR BEFORE MAY 1, 1933

all GOLD COIN, GOLD BULLION, AND GOLD CERTIFICATES now owned by them to a Federal Reserve Bank, branch or agency, or to any member bank of the Federal Reserve System.

Executive Order

FORBIDDING THE HOARDING OF GOLD COIN, GOLD BULLION AND GOLD CERTIFICATES

Illustration 23: Executive Order 6102 published on April 5, 1933.

Some bitcoin supporters have warned that bitcoin could get the same treatment if it becomes too big of a "problem." Of course, the nature of bitcoin makes it much more difficult for the government to enforce such an act. Bitcoin is a completely digital asset, it does not exist in physical form, and its possession is equivalent to the possession of the private key or seed phrase that allows it to be transferred. Confiscating bitcoins would consist of forcing their holders to transfer them or hand over their private keys. The immaterial nature of bitcoin would allow its holders to move to a more favorable country, carrying their bitcoins easily. To do this, they only need to memorize a private key or a set of 12 or 24 words. This is one of the properties that makes bitcoin a better store of value.

The truth is that big changes have always produced fear, skepticism, and contrary positions. The steam engine, electricity, the car, or the Internet are clear examples of this. At the time they suffered the same type of criticism and opposing positions as Bitcoin.

Illustration 24: Propaganda posters against electricity or combustion vehicles.

Conclusion

In theory, some governments could try to ban or shut
down Bitcoin. However, in practice, this would be ex-
tremely difficult due to the decentralized nature of the
cryptocurrency. As a global, decentralized network,
there is no single entity or authority that controls
Bitcoin.

Furthermore, the decentralized nature of Bitcoin
also makes it difficult for any government to fully control or regulate its use. Although a government could
try to restrict or limit Bitcoin transactions, it would be
difficult to impose these restrictions worldwide. A
Bitcoin ban could also have negative economic and social consequences, such as job losses and increased
criminal activity. In addition, it could lead to mistrust
in the government and financial institutions, and be in-
effective in reducing the use and possession of Bitcoin
due to the decentralized nature of the cryptocurrency.

And while some governments might decide to restrict or ban the use of Bitcoin, others will likely choose
to take the opposite position, embracing and facilitat-
ing its adoption, taking advantage of the positive effects that Bitcoin can bring to their country and its
citizens. This favorable stance towards Bitcoin, despite
the risks involved, also presents a great opportunity
and would place these governments and countries in
an unrepeatable advantageous competitive position.

REFERENCES

Aderinokun et al. (2022, 06 14). *Letter in Support of Responsible Crypto Policy*. Retrieved from https://www.financialinclusion.tech/

Antonopoulos, AM (2017). *Internet of Money*. Merkle Bloom LLC.

Boyapati, V. (2018, March 2). *The Bullish Case for Bitcoin*. Retrieved from Medium: https://vijayboyapati.medium.com/the-bullish-case-for-bitcoin-6ecc8bdecc1

Carter, N. (2019). *Ten Years of Bitcoin: Evaluating Its Performance as a Monetary System*.

chainanalysis. (2022). *Crypto Crime Trends for 2022*.

CNMV. (2022). *Scams and fraud. CNMV Guide*.

Donald, JA (2008, November 2). Re: Bitcoin P2P e-cash paper. Email to Satoshi.

European Union Agency for Criminal Justice Cooperation. (2022, 10 22). *Money laundering cases registered at Agency doubled in last 6 years according to Eurojust's new report*. Retrieved from Eurojust: https://www.eurojust.europa.eu/news/money-laundering-cases-registered-agency-doubled-last-6-years-according-eurojusts-new-report#:~:text=The %20United%20Nations%20Office%20on,Eu

ros%20%2D%20is%20laundered%20each%2
0year.

Fidelity Digital Assets. (2022, 01). *Bitcoin First: Why investors need to consider bitcoin.* Retrieved from https://www.fidelitydigitalassets.com/sites/d efault/files/documents/bitcoin-first.pdf

Gladstein, A. (2022). *Check your Financial Privilege.* BTC Media LLC.

Investopedia. (2022, 09). *Intrinsic Value Defined and How It's Determined in Investing and Business.* Retrieved from https://www.investopedia.com/terms/i/intri nsicvalue.asp

Major, J. (2022, 09 15). *7 facts from Michael Saylor why Bitcoin mining is cleanest industrial use of electricity.* Retrieved from Finbold: https://finbold.com/7-facts-from-michael-saylor-why-bitcoin-mining-is-cleanest-industrial-use-of-electricity/

Nakamoto, S. (2008, 11 08). *Bitcoin P2P e-cash paper.* Retrieved from Cryptography Mailing List.

Nakamoto, S. (2008, October 31). *Bitcoin: A Peer-to-Peer Electronic Cash System.* Retrieved from bitcoin.org: http://www.bitcoin.org/bitcoin.pdf

Nakamoto, S. (2009, 12 10). *Re: Questions about Bitcoin.* Retrieved from BitcoinTalk.

Nakamoto, S. (2010, 08 07). *Re: Bitcoin minting is thermodynamically perverse.* Retrieved from BitcoinTalk.

Nakamoto, S. (2010, 08 07). *Re: Bitcoins are most like shares of common stock.* Retrieved from BitcoinTalk.

Nakamoto, S. (2010, July 5). *Re: Slashdot Submission for 1.0.* Retrieved from Bitcoin Forum: https://bitcointalk.org/index.php?topic=234. msg1976#msg1976

Nakamoto, S. (2010, 02 14). *Re: What's with this odd generation?* Retrieved from BitcoinTalk.

NewLibertyStandard. (2009). *2009 Exchange Rate.* Retrieved from https://web.archive.org/web/200912291326 10/https://newlibertystandard.wetpaint.com/ page/Exchange+Rate

Poon, J., & Dryja, T. (2016). *The Bitcoin Lightning Network: Scalable Off-Chain Instant Payments.*

Sagan, C. (1979).

Saylor, M. (2022, 10 18). *Twitter.* Retrieved from https://twitter.com/saylor/status/158246204 5144125443?s=20

Tully, S. (2021, 10 27). *Fortune.*

INDEX OF ILLUSTRATIONS

SIf something is evident, it is that Bitcoin does not leave anyone indifferent. Bitcoin has a large number of supporters and detractors, whose positions are sometimes based on solid arguments, and at other times based solely on headlines and persistent myths.

The truth is that Bitcoin has been the subject of misunderstandings and a multitude of criticisms and unfair judgments since the publication of its white paper fourteen years ago.

Does Bitcoin have intrinsic value? Is it a fraud or a pyramid scheme? Does it waste energy? Is your security model sustainable? It's too slow? You can scale? Is it used for illegal purposes? Will it be replaced by another cryptocurrency? Will it be shut down or banned?

Debunking Common Bitcoin Criticisms is a compendium of analysis of the most common and recurring criticisms of Bitcoin. These analyzes are the result of years of study and learning trying to find the truth.

Álvaro Suárez is a computer engineer and has a master's degree in Computer Science. He has been developing and leading innovative projects in the Bitcoin ecosystem for years. He has also been teaching and training professionals on Bitcoin since 2018.

He is also the author of the book *The Fundamentals of Bitcoin*.

ISBN 9798392487752

90000

9 798392 487752